CLASSIC

Appetizers

HOME COOKING

Publications International, Ltd.
Favorite Brand Name Recipes at www.fbnr.com

Pictured on the front cover: Sweet Hot Chicken Wings *(page 60).*

ISBN: 0-7853-7803-0

Manufactured in China.

8 7 6 5 4 3 2 1

Microwave Cooking: Microwave ovens vary in wattage. Use the cooking times as guidelines and check for doneness before adding more time.

The publisher would like to thank the following companies and organizations for the use of their recipes in this publication: National Sunflower Association *(page 50);* Sargento® Foods Inc. *(page 18);* Unilever Bestfoods North America *(page 12);* Wisconsin Milk Marketing Board *(pages 38 and 48).*

CONTENTS

Picante Black Bean Soup *(page 10)*

Clams Casino *(page 54)*

Sweet Hot Chicken Wings *(page 60)*

CLASS NOTES

Appetizers, hors d'oeuvres, finger foods—whichever term you use, these tasty tidbits do much more than just tide guests over until dinner. In fact, the word hors d'oeuvres means "outside the main meal"—they set the stage for the meal that is to follow. These delicious appetite enhancers are versatile enough to provide party sustenance on their own at an open house, satisfy cravings for midnight munchies or just awaken the appetite in a refreshing first course. However you decide to serve them, appetizers are meant to be enjoyed by both the guests and the cook. The preparation of these menu additions need not be overwhelming. Some simple, up-front planning combined with the step-by-step recipes in *Cooking Class Appetizers* will help to maintain the cook's composure and create a relaxed, festive atmosphere.

When serving appetizers before a meal, keep in mind they are meant to tease the appetite, not satisfy it. One or two selections should be ample, allowing five to seven servings per person. Prepare recipes that contrast in texture, temperature and flavor with the meal that follows. For example, a cold seafood hors d'oeuvre would be a refreshing opener before a main course highlighting roast beef or steak. However, if you are planning an ethnic dinner, coordinating an appetizer from the same foreign country provides a memorable beginning. Many people prefer to serve first-course appetizers before the guests are seated at the dinner table, as this allows the cook time to make last-minute meal preparations. However, starters such as soups and marinated salads should always be served when guests are seated.

For a cocktail party or open house where appetizers are served as the main event, plan a variety of snacks and spreads, including some that are hearty and filling. Remember, too, that the longer the occasion lasts, the more your guests will eat. Plan on ten to twelve servings per person as a minimum. Cold appetizers, such as dips and marinated vegetables, should be made at least several hours to one day ahead since their flavor actually improves with time. Some hot appetizers can be cooked ahead and simply reheated just before serving, while others must be prepared at the last moment. Be sure to enlist kitchen help, if necessary, to give these final details the attention they require. If the food on your appetizer table will be sitting out for several hours, it is important, for food safety reasons, to maintain serving temperatures. Appetizers that need to remain chilled, such as shrimp cocktail, should be served on a platter set over cracked ice. Transfer hot appetizers, such as meatballs, from the oven or rangetop to a warming device, such as a chafing dish or fondue pot for serving. Prepare a balance of hot and cold appetizers that provide a range of flavors and textures, from spicy and rich to light and refreshing. And keep in mind that at a large party where seating is limited, guests appreciate finger food and bite-size portions with not-too-drippy sauces.

Following are a few suggestions for first-course appetizers and some easy and delicious entertaining ideas. The football party and open house menus can easily be supplemented with a deli tray or thinly sliced ham, depending on the number of guests and the length of the party. You may wish to serve a variety of flavored coffees and an assortment of delightful cookies as the gathering draws to a close.

First-Course Starters
(Serve any one of the following recipes)
Sherried Oyster and Brie Soup (page 16)
Elegant Shrimp Scampi (page 22)
Chilly Cucumber Soup (page 12)
Chinese Vegetable Rolls (page 32)

Midnight Movie Munchies
Cheesy Sun Crisps (page 50)
Harvest-Time Popcorn (page 52)
Oven-Fried California Quesadillas (page 46)
Chicken 'n' Rice Pizza (page 44)

Fall Football Party
Taco Dip (page 38)
Sweet Hot Chicken Wings (page 60)
Cheesy Snack Squares (page 42)
Cheesy Onion Focaccia (page 29)

Holiday Open House
Microwave Oriental Relish Dip (page 40)
Spinach-Feta Triangles (page 26)
Sesame-Sour Cream Meatballs (page 57)
Egg Champignons (page 24)

Black-Eyed Pea Soup

2 pounds dried East Texas Black-Eyed Peas
2 large potatoes
4 medium onions, thinly sliced (page 29)
4 carrots, thinly sliced
½ pound bacon, diced (page 10)
8 quarts water
2 cups thinly sliced celery
2 whole jalapeño peppers
4 bay leaves
½ teaspoon dried thyme leaves, crushed
1 meaty ham bone
  Salt and black pepper to taste

1. Rinse black-eyed peas under cold running water. Drain and set aside.

2. To grate potatoes, remove potato skins with paring knife or vegetable peeler. Grate potatoes using medium holes on a box-shaped grater. Place grated potatoes in large bowl of ice water. Set aside.

3. Combine onions, carrots and bacon in large stockpot. Cook and stir over medium-high heat until onions are golden.

4. Drain potatoes. Add black-eyed peas, water, potatoes, celery, jalapeño peppers, bay leaves, thyme and ham bone to onion mixture. Season with salt and black pepper. Bring to a boil. Reduce heat to low. Simmer, covered, 3 to 4 hours. Remove and discard jalapeño peppers and bay leaves.

5. Remove ham bone from soup. Let stand at room temperature until cool enough to handle. Cut meat from ham bone and chop into bite-size pieces. Return meat to stockpot.

6. Adjust seasonings; reheat if necessary.

Makes 12 to 16 servings

Picante Black Bean Soup

4 slices bacon
1 large onion
1 clove garlic, minced
   (page 36)
2 cans (15 ounces each)
   black beans,
   undrained
1 can (about 14 ounces)
   beef broth
1¼ cups water
¾ cup picante sauce
½ to 1 teaspoon salt
½ teaspoon dried oregano
   leaves, crushed
   Sour cream
   Crackers and additional
   picante sauce for
   serving

1. Using scissors, cut through several slices of bacon at once, cutting into ½ × ½-inch pieces. Set aside.

2. Peel skin from onion; cut in half through the root. Place, cut side down, on cutting board. To coarsely chop onion, hold knife horizontally. Make cuts parallel to board, almost to root end. Make vertical, lengthwise cuts of desired thickness. Slice across cuts to root end. (The closer the cuts are spaced, the finer the onion is chopped.) Set aside.

3. Cook and stir bacon in Dutch oven over medium-high heat until crisp. Remove with slotted spoon; drain on paper towels. Set bacon aside.

4. Add onion and garlic to drippings in Dutch oven; cook and stir 3 minutes.

5. Add beans with liquid, broth, water, ¾ cup picante sauce, salt and oregano. Bring to a boil. Reduce heat to low. Simmer, covered, 20 minutes.

6. Ladle into soup bowls; dollop with sour cream. Sprinkle with bacon. Serve with crackers and additional picante sauce.

Makes 6 to 8 servings

Chilly Cucumber Soup

4 large cucumbers
2 tablespoons butter or
margarine
2 tablespoons all-purpose
flour
¼ cup finely chopped
fresh parsley
¼ cup finely chopped
celery leaves
1 envelope LIPTON®
RECIPE SECRETS®
Golden Onion Soup
Mix
2 cups water
2 cups light cream or half-
and-half
Cucumber slices, celery
leaves and lemon peel
for garnish

1. Remove cucumber peels with paring knife or vegetable peeler. To seed cucumbers, cut in half lengthwise and scrape out seeds with a small spoon. Finely chop enough cucumbers to measure 3½ cups. Set aside.

2. Melt butter in large saucepan over medium heat. Stir in flour and cook 3 minutes, stirring constantly.

3. Add chopped cucumbers, parsley and chopped celery leaves. Reduce heat to low. Cook and stir until cucumbers are tender when pierced with fork, about 8 minutes.

4. Combine soup mix and water in small bowl; add to cucumber mixture. Bring to a boil over medium-high heat. Reduce heat to low. Simmer, covered, 15 minutes. Remove from heat. Let stand at room temperature until cool.

5. Process soup in small batches in blender or food processor until smooth.

6. Stir cream into soup. Cover; refrigerate. Serve soup cold. Garnish, if desired.
Makes about 6 servings

"Dearhearts" Seafood Bisque

1 pound mixed shellfish
(raw shrimp, raw
scallops or canned
crabmeat)
2 tablespoons olive oil
1 onion, finely chopped
1 (9-ounce) package
frozen artichoke
hearts, thawed
2 cups chicken broth
½ cup white wine
1 cup heavy or whipping
cream
2 tablespoons chopped
fresh parsley
1 teaspoon salt
½ teaspoon ground
nutmeg
¼ teaspoon white pepper
Additional chopped
fresh parsley for
garnish

1. To remove shells from shrimp, use your fingers to peel shell off the side with the legs. Lift it up and over, then back around to the leg side. Discard shells. Using paring knife, cut off and discard tail sections.

2. To devein shrimp, use paring knife to make a small cut along the back of the shrimp; lift out the dark vein with knife tip. (You may find this easier to do under cold running water.) Cut each shrimp into 3 to 4 smaller pieces, if desired. Set shrimp aside.

3. Heat oil in large skillet over medium-high heat. Add onion; cook and stir 5 minutes or until softened. Add artichokes, broth and wine. Bring to a boil over medium-high heat. Reduce heat to low. Simmer, covered, 5 to 7 minutes.

4. Process soup in small batches in food processor or blender until smooth. Return soup to saucepan.

5. Stir in shellfish, heavy cream, 2 tablespoons chopped parsley, salt, nutmeg and pepper. Bring soup just to a simmer over medium heat. Reduce heat to low. Simmer very gently, uncovered, 5 to 10 minutes. Do not boil. (Shellfish will become tough if soup boils.) Garnish, if desired.

Makes 6 servings

Sherried Oyster and Brie Soup

1 cup cream sherry
1 quart select Maryland
    oysters with liquor
2 tablespoons butter
1 pound fresh
    mushrooms, thinly
    sliced
½ cup minced shallots
2 tablespoons fresh
    lemon juice
2 tablespoons all-purpose
    flour
3 cups beef broth
4 ounces Brie cheese
1 cup milk
1 cup heavy or whipping
    cream
    Salt and white pepper to
    taste
    Fresh chives for garnish

1. Bring sherry to a boil in small saucepan over medium-high heat. Reduce heat to low. Simmer until slightly thickened and reduced to ½ cup. Set aside.

2. Drain oysters and reserve liquor. Set aside.

3. Melt butter in large saucepan over medium-high heat. When foam subsides, stir in mushrooms, shallots and lemon juice; cook and stir 2 minutes. Sprinkle with flour; cook and stir 1 minute more.

4. Add broth and reduced sherry; bring to a boil over medium-high heat. Reduce heat to low. Simmer 20 minutes.

5. Cut Brie cheese into wedges and, using paring knife, remove and discard outer white rind.

6. Add cheese to soup; stir to melt. Stir in reserved oyster liquor, milk and cream; season with salt and pepper. Heat until very hot. Do not boil.

7. Remove from heat; add oysters. Cover and let stand until oysters are just plumped. Garnish, if desired.

Makes 4 servings

Cheddar Chili Tomato Pots

6 medium tomatoes
3½ cups (14 ounces) Sargento® Fancy Sharp Cheddar Shredded Cheese, divided
2 cans (4 ounces each) chopped green chilies, well drained
½ teaspoon dried oregano leaves, crushed
½ teaspoon minced garlic (page 36)
6 tablespoons sour cream
3 green onions, sliced
Breadsticks for serving

1. Preheat oven to 325°F. Grease 11×7-inch baking dish. Cut ½-inch slice from top of each tomato; scoop out pulp and seeds, leaving ¼-inch shell (save pulp for another use, such as salads or sauces).

2. Invert tomatoes on paper towel-lined plate; let drain 20 minutes.

3. Combine 3 cups cheese, chilies, oregano and garlic in medium bowl.

4. Using large spoon, stuff tomato shells with cheese mixture.

5. Arrange tomato shells in prepared dish. Bake 20 minutes. Top with sour cream, remaining ½ cup cheese and green onions. Serve with breadsticks.

Makes 6 first-course servings

Jumbo Shells Seafood Fancies

1 package (16 ounces)
    uncooked jumbo
    pasta shells
1 can (7½ ounces)
    crabmeat
4 ounces (1 cup) grated
    Swiss cheese
1 can (2½ ounces) tiny
    shrimp, drained
½ cup salad dressing or
    mayonnaise
2 tablespoons thinly
    sliced celery
1 tablespoon finely
    chopped onion
1 tablespoon finely
    chopped pimiento
    Celery leaves for
    garnish

1. Cook shells according to package directions until tender but still firm; drain. Rinse under cold running water; drain again.

2. Invert shells on paper towel-lined plate to drain and cool.

3. Drain and discard liquid from crabmeat. Place crabmeat in large bowl; flake with fork into small pieces. Remove any bits of shell or cartilage.

4. Add Swiss cheese, shrimp, salad dressing, celery, onion and pimiento to crabmeat. If mixture seems too dry, add more salad dressing.

5. Using large spoon, stuff cooled shells with seafood mixture. Cover; refrigerate until chilled. Garnish, if desired.

Makes 8 first-course servings

Elegant Shrimp Scampi

1½ pounds large raw
    prawns (about 14)
6 tablespoons butter
4 tablespoons minced
    garlic (page 36)
6 green onions, thinly
    sliced
¼ cup dry white wine
    Juice of 1 lemon (about
    2 tablespoons)
8 large fresh parsley
    sprigs, finely chopped
Salt and black pepper to
    taste
Lemon slices and fresh
    parsley sprigs for
    garnish

1. To remove shells from prawns, use your fingers to peel shell off the side with the legs. Lift it up and over, then back around to the leg side. Discard shells. Do not cut off tail section.

2. To devein prawns, use paring knife to make a small cut along the back of the prawns; lift out the dark vein with knife tip. (You may find this easier to do under cold running water.) Set prawns aside.

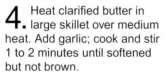

3. To clarify butter, melt butter in small saucepan over low heat. Do not stir. Skim off the white foam that forms on top. Strain clarified butter through a cheesecloth into glass measuring cup to yield ⅓ cup. Discard milky residue at bottom of pan.

4. Heat clarified butter in large skillet over medium heat. Add garlic; cook and stir 1 to 2 minutes until softened but not brown.

5. Add prawns, green onions, wine and lemon juice; cook and stir until prawns turn pink and are firm and opaque, 1 to 2 minutes on each side. Do not overcook.

6. Just before serving, add chopped parsley and season with salt and pepper. Serve on individual shell-shaped or small gratin dishes. Garnish, if desired.

Makes 8 first-course servings

Egg Champignons

6 eggs
¼ cup dry bread crumbs
¼ cup (1 ounce) crumbled
blue cheese
2 tablespoons thinly
sliced green onions
with tops
2 tablespoons dry white
wine
2 tablespoons butter,
melted
1 tablespoon chopped
fresh parsley *or*
½ tablespoon dried
parsley flakes
½ teaspoon garlic salt
24 large fresh mushroom
caps (about
1½ inches in
diameter)
Paprika (optional)
Green onions and
tomato slices for
garnish

1. To hard cook eggs, place the 6 eggs in a single layer in a saucepan. Add enough water to cover eggs by at least 1 inch. Cover and quickly bring water just to a boil over high heat. Turn off heat. If necessary, remove the pan from burner to prevent further boiling. Let eggs stand, covered, in hot water 15 to 17 minutes. Immediately run cold water over eggs or place in ice water until completely cooled.

2. Peel eggs by tapping all around the shell with a table knife to form a network of cracks. Peel shell away under cold running water. Finely chop eggs.

3. Preheat oven to 450°F. Lightly grease baking sheet. Combine eggs, bread crumbs, blue cheese, 2 tablespoons green onions, wine, butter, parsley and garlic salt in medium bowl.

4. Fill each mushroom cap with 1 rounded tablespoon egg mixture. Place mushroom caps on prepared baking sheet.

5. Bake 8 to 10 minutes. Sprinkle with paprika. Garnish, if desired.

Makes 8 first-course servings

Spinach-Feta Triangles

1 small onion
½ cup minced fresh
    parsley
3 packages (10 ounces
    each) frozen chopped
    spinach, thawed
¼ cup olive oil
2 eggs
16 ounces (1 pound) feta
    cheese, drained and
    crumbled
1 teaspoon dried oregano
    leaves, crushed *or*
    2 tablespoons
    chopped fresh
    oregano leaves
    Freshly grated nutmeg
    to taste
    Salt and black pepper to
    taste
1 package (16 ounces)
    frozen phyllo dough,
    thawed to room
    temperature
2 cups margarine, melted

1. To chop onion in food processor, peel and quarter onion; place in bowl. Pulse 4 to 7 times until onion is finely chopped. Scrape bowl once during chopping. Chop enough onion to measure ½ cup. Drain onions, if needed. Set aside. (See page 10 for chopping technique with knife.)

2. To mince parsley, place parsley in 1-cup measuring cup. Snip enough parsley with kitchen scissors to measure ½ cup. Set aside.

3. To drain spinach, place spinach, 1 package at a time, in bottom of pie plate. Place another pie plate on top; over sink squeeze plates together and tilt slightly to press excess liquid from spinach. Set spinach aside.

4. Preheat oven to 375°F.

5. Heat oil over medium-high heat in small skillet. Add onion; cook and stir until translucent and golden.

6. Beat eggs in large bowl with an electric mixer at medium-high speed until light and lemon colored.

7. Stir in onion with oil, feta cheese, parsley, oregano and spinach. Season with nutmeg, salt and pepper.

continued on page 28

Spinach-Feta Triangles, continued

8. Remove phyllo from package; unroll and place on large sheet of waxed paper. Fold phyllo crosswise into thirds. Use scissors to cut along folds into thirds.

9. Cover phyllo with large sheet of plastic wrap and damp, clean kitchen towel. (Phyllo dries out quickly if not covered.)

10. Lay 1 strip of phyllo at a time on a flat surface and brush immediately with melted butter. Fold strip in half lengthwise. Brush with butter again. Place rounded teaspoonful of spinach filling on 1 end of strip; fold over 1 corner to make triangle.

11. Continue folding end to end, as you would fold a flag, keeping edges straight.

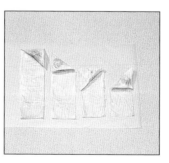

12. Brush top with butter. Repeat process until all filling is used up.

13. Place triangles in a single layer, seam-side down, on ungreased jelly-roll pan. Bake 20 minutes or until lightly browned. Serve warm.

Makes 5 dozen appetizers

Cheesy Onion Focaccia

1 large red onion
½ cup plus 3 tablespoons honey, divided
2⅓ cups warm water (105° to 115°F), divided
1½ packages active dry yeast
6 tablespoons olive oil, divided
⅓ cup cornmeal
3 cups whole wheat flour
1½ tablespoons coarse salt
3 to 4 cups all-purpose flour, divided
1 cup red wine vinegar
Additional cornmeal
1 cup grated Parmesan cheese
½ teaspoon onion salt
Black pepper to taste

1. To slice onion, peel skin and cut onion in half through the root. Place, cut side down, on cutting board. Cut thin, vertical slices the length of the onion. Set aside.

2. To proof yeast, place 3 tablespoons honey in large bowl. Pour ⅓ cup water over honey. Do not stir. Sprinkle yeast over water. Let stand at room temperature about 15 minutes or until bubbly.*

3. Add remaining 2 cups water, 3 tablespoons olive oil, ⅓ cup cornmeal and whole wheat flour to yeast mixture; mix until well blended.

4. Stir in salt and 2 cups all-purpose flour. Gradually stir in enough remaining all-purpose flour until mixture clings to sides of bowl.

5. Turn dough out onto lightly floured surface. To knead in remaining flour, fold the dough in half toward you and press dough away from you with heels of hands. Give dough a quarter turn and continue folding, pushing and turning until the dough is smooth and satiny, about 10 minutes.

continued on page 30

Cheesy Onion Focaccia, continued

6. Divide dough into halves. Place each half in a large, lightly greased bowl; turn each dough half over to grease surface. Cover each with clean kitchen towel and let dough rise in warm place (85°F) until doubled in bulk. (Press two fingertips about ½ inch into dough. Dough is ready if indentations remain when fingers are removed.)

7. Meanwhile, combine onion, vinegar and remaining ½ cup honey. Marinate at room temperature at least 1 hour.

8. Grease 2 (12-inch) pizza pans and sprinkle with additional cornmeal. Stretch dough and pat into pans; create valleys with fingertips.

9. Cover dough with greased plastic wrap; let rise for 1 hour. Dough will double in size.

10. Preheat oven to 400°F.

11. Drain onions and scatter them over dough. Sprinkle with remaining 3 tablespoons olive oil, Parmesan cheese and onion salt; season with pepper.

12. Bake 25 to 30 minutes until flatbread is crusty and golden. Cut into wedges to serve. Serve warm.

Makes 2 breads (6 to 8 servings each)

*If yeast does not bubble, it is no longer active. Discard yeast mixture and start again. Always check the expiration date on yeast packet. Also, water that is too hot will kill yeast; it is best to use a thermometer.

Chinese Vegetable Rolls

¼ cup red wine
2 tablespoons teriyaki
sauce
2 tablespoons
Worcestershire sauce
1 cup diced zucchini
1 cup diced yellow
squash
1 cup small broccoli
flowerets
1 cup small cauliflower
flowerets
½ cup diced carrots
¼ cup chopped red onion
(page 10)
¼ cup chopped fresh
parsley
¼ teaspoon white pepper
¼ teaspoon garlic salt
⅛ teaspoon ground red
pepper
⅛ teaspoon black pepper
1 package (16 ounces)
egg roll wrappers
1 egg, beaten
Peanut or corn oil for
frying
Sweet and sour sauce,
hot mustard sauce or
soy sauce for dipping

1. Combine wine, teriyaki sauce and Worcestershire sauce in large saucepan in large saucepan over medium heat. Stir in zucchini, squash, broccoli, cauliflower, carrots, red onion, parsley, white pepper, garlic salt, ground red pepper and black pepper. Cook and stir 5 to 6 minutes until flavors blend and vegetables are crisp-tender. Do not overcook.

2. Remove from heat. Immediately transfer vegetable mixture to bowl to prevent further cooking. Let stand at room temperature until cool.

3. Place about 2 tablespoons vegetable mixture on bottom half of 1 egg roll wrapper.

4. Moisten left and right edges of wrapper with egg. Fold bottom edge up to just cover filling.

5. Fold left and right edges over ½ inch; roll up jelly-roll fashion.

6. Moisten top edge with egg to seal. Repeat with remaining egg roll wrappers and vegetable filling.

7. Heat ½ inch oil in large, heavy saucepan over medium-high heat until oil reaches 365°F; adjust heat to maintain temperature. Fry egg rolls, a few at a time, in hot oil 2 minutes or until golden brown, turning once. Remove with slotted spoon; drain on paper towels.

8. Serve warm with sauces for dipping.

Makes about 15 appetizers

Serbian Lamb Sausage Kabobs

1 pound lean ground lamb
1 pound lean ground beef
1 small onion, finely
  chopped (page 10)
2 cloves garlic, minced
  (page 36)
1 tablespoon hot
  Hungarian paprika
1 small egg, slightly
  beaten
  Salt and black pepper to
  taste
3 to 4 red, green or yellow
  bell peppers, cut into
  squares
  Rice pilaf for serving
  Tomato slices and green
  onion brushes for
  garnish

1. Combine lamb, beef, finely chopped onion, garlic, paprika and egg in large bowl; season with salt and black pepper.

2. Place meat mixture on cutting board; pat evenly into 8×6-inch rectangle. With sharp knife, cut meat into 48 (1-inch) squares; shape each square into small oblong sausage.

3. Place sausages on waxed paper-lined jelly-roll pan and freeze 30 to 45 minutes or until firm. Do not freeze completely.

4. Alternately thread 3 sausages and 3 bell pepper pieces onto each metal skewer.

5. Grill over medium-hot coals 5 to 7 minutes. Turn kabobs, taking care not to knock sausages off. Continue grilling 5 to 7 minutes longer until meat is done. Serve with rice pilaf.

6. For green onion brushes, trim root and most of green top from green onions. Using sharp scissors, make parallel cuts, about 1½ inches long, along length of each onion at the root end or both ends. Fan out the cuts to form a brush. If desired, place brushes in bowl of ice water for several hours to open and curl. Place green onion brush and several tomato slices on each plate, if desired.

Makes 8 servings or 16 kabobs

Note: The seasonings may be adjusted, but the key to authenticity is the equal parts of beef and lamb and the garlic and paprika. You may use sweet paprika if you prefer a milder taste.

Patrician Escargots

4 heads garlic,* separated into cloves
½ cup olive oil
½ cup butter
1 onion, finely chopped (page 10)
1 teaspoon finely chopped fresh rosemary leaves *or* ½ teaspoon dried rosemary leaves, crushed
¼ teaspoon dried thyme leaves, crushed
2 dashes ground nutmeg
Salt and black pepper to taste
24 large canned snails, drained
½ cup chopped fresh parsley
24 large fresh mushrooms
12 pieces thin-sliced white bread for serving

1. Trim off ends of garlic cloves. To loosen garlic peels, crush cloves with flat side of a large knife. Remove peels and discard.** Finely chop garlic.

2. Heat oil and butter in large skillet over medium heat until butter is melted. Add garlic, onion, rosemary, thyme and nutmeg; season with salt and pepper. Reduce heat to low. Add snails and parsley to garlic mixture. Cook 30 minutes, stirring occasionally.

3. Preheat oven to 350°F. Remove stems from mushrooms and discard.

4. Arrange mushroom caps upside down in 2-inch-deep baking dish; place 1 snail from garlic mixture in each mushroom cap. Pour garlic mixture over snails; cover with foil and bake 30 minutes.

5. Meanwhile, remove crusts from bread slices. Toast each slice and cut diagonally into 4 triangles. Serve with escargots.

Makes 4 servings

*The whole garlic bulb is called a head.

**To peel garlic cloves in microwave, place the desired number of cloves in small custard cup. Microwave at HIGH (100% power) until slightly softened, 5 to 10 seconds for 1 clove or 45 to 55 seconds for a whole head. Slip the cloves out of their skins.

Taco Dip

12 ounces cream cheese,
  softened
½ cup dairy sour cream
2 teaspoons chili powder
1½ teaspoons ground
  cumin
⅛ teaspoon ground red
  pepper
½ cup salsa
  Crisp salad greens
1 cup (4 ounces)
  shredded Wisconsin
  Cheddar cheese
1 cup (4 ounces)
  shredded Wisconsin
  Monterey Jack cheese
½ cup diced plum
  tomatoes
⅓ cup sliced green onions
¼ cup sliced pitted ripe
  olives
¼ cup sliced pimiento-
  stuffed green olives
  Tortilla chips and blue
  corn chips for serving

1. Combine cream cheese, sour cream, chili powder, cumin and ground red pepper in large bowl; mix until well blended. Stir in salsa.

2. Spread dip onto greens-lined 10-inch serving platter.

3. Top with Cheddar cheese, Monterey Jack cheese, tomatoes, green onions, ripe olives and green olives.

4. Serve with tortilla chips and blue corn chips.

Makes 10 servings

Note: Blue corn chips are made from special corn hybrids. The kernels appear almost black in color. Because blue hybrids tend to have low yields, products made from them are more expensive.

Microwave Oriental Relish Dip

1 cup peeled, chopped tomatoes
¼ cup soy sauce
¼ cup drained canned crushed pineapple
1 tablespoon firmly packed brown sugar
1 tablespoon finely chopped red bell pepper
1 tablespoon finely chopped green onion
1 tablespoon minced garlic (page 36)
2 teaspoons fresh lime juice
1½ teaspoons grated fresh ginger (page 60)
2 teaspoons rice wine vinegar
1 teaspoon sesame oil
1 teaspoon arrowroot or **1½ teaspoons cornstarch**
2 teaspoons cold water
2 (8-ounce) packages cream cheese, softened
1 cup canned cream of coconut
1 cup creamy peanut butter
2 tablespoons fresh lime juice
¼ teaspoon ground red pepper
¼ teaspoon ground cardamom
8 cups assorted fresh vegetables for serving

1. Combine tomatoes, soy sauce, pineapple, sugar, bell pepper, onion, garlic, 2 teaspoons lime juice and ginger in 1-quart glass measuring cup.

2. Microwave at HIGH (100% power) 8 minutes, stirring every 2 minutes. Stir in vinegar and oil. Microwave 5 to 6 minutes until tomato mixture is reduced to 1 cup.

3. Combine arrowroot and water in small dish; stir until well blended. Add to tomato mixture; stir well. Let stand at room temperature to cool slightly. Store relish, covered, in glass container in refrigerator.

4. To make dip, combine cream cheese and cream of coconut in large bowl; add relish and peanut butter. Mix until thoroughly combined. Add 2 tablespoons lime juice, ground red pepper and cardamom; stir until well blended. Serve with assorted vegetables.

Makes 16 servings

Note: Relish is also great mixed with reduced-calorie mayonnaise and used as a sandwich spread or salad dressing.

Cheesy Snack Squares

1¼ cups all-purpose flour
½ cup thinly sliced green onions
¾ cup corn meal
1 tablespoon sugar
2 teaspoons baking powder
1 teaspoon dried Italian seasoning
¼ teaspoon salt
1 cup milk
¼ cup vegetable oil
1 egg
1 cup (4 ounces) shredded Cheddar cheese
1 can (4 ounces) chopped green chilies, well drained
¼ cup finely chopped red bell pepper
2 slices crisp-cooked bacon, crumbled

1. Preheat oven to 400°F. Grease 11×7-inch baking dish. Combine flour, green onions, corn meal, sugar, baking powder, Italian seasoning and salt in large bowl; mix well.

2. Combine milk, oil and egg in small bowl. Add to corn meal mixture; mix just until moistened.

3. Spread evenly into prepared dish.

4. Combine cheese, chilies, bell pepper and bacon in medium bowl. Sprinkle evenly over corn meal mixture.

5. Bake 25 to 30 minutes until wooden toothpick inserted into center comes out clean. Let stand at room temperature to cool 10 minutes before cutting.

Makes about 15 pieces

Note: Also great served as a side dish to fish, chicken or pork—just cut into 8 pieces.

Chicken 'n' Rice Pizza

4 cups cooked rice
½ cup ground walnuts
(optional)
1½ cups (6 ounces)
shredded Swiss
cheese, divided
½ cup grated Parmesan
cheese, divided
1 egg, beaten
2 tablespoons olive oil
2 boneless skinless
chicken breast halves
(about 6 ounces
each), cut into bite-
size pieces
1 small onion, sliced
(page 29)
½ green bell pepper, sliced
½ red bell pepper, sliced
¼ pound fresh
mushrooms, sliced
½ cup sliced pitted ripe
olives
1 jar (14 ounces) pizza
sauce
1 teaspoon dried basil
leaves, crushed
1 teaspoon dried oregano
leaves, crushed
1 cup (4 ounces)
shredded mozzarella
cheese

1. Preheat oven to 375°F.
Combine rice, walnuts,
½ cup Swiss cheese, ¼ cup
Parmesan cheese and egg in
large bowl.

2. Press rice mixture evenly
onto bottom and ½ inch
up side of greased 14-inch
pizza pan. Bake 10 minutes.
Let stand at room temperature
until cool.

3. Heat oil in large skillet
over medium-high heat.
Add chicken, onion, bell
peppers, mushrooms and
olives. Cook and stir 7 minutes
or until chicken is no longer
pink in center; drain off
excess liquid.

4. Spread pizza sauce over
cooled rice crust. Spread
remaining 1 cup Swiss
cheese over sauce. Spread
chicken mixture over cheese.
Sprinkle with herbs.

5. Top pizza with
mozzarella cheese and
remaining ¼ cup Parmesan
cheese. Bake 15 to 20
minutes. Remove from oven.
Let stand at room temperature
to cool slightly before serving.

*Makes about 16 appetizer
servings or 6 main-dish
servings*

Oven-Fried California Quesadillas

½ cup chopped almonds
2½ cups (10 ounces)
    shredded Monterey
    Jack cheese
1 jar (6 ounces) marinated
    artichoke hearts,
    drained and chopped
1 can (2¼ ounces) sliced
    pitted ripe olives,
    drained
⅔ cup picante sauce
¼ cup loosely packed,
    chopped cilantro
8 flour tortillas (7 to 8
    inch), divided
3 tablespoons butter or
    margarine, melted
Additional picante
    sauce
Lime wedges for
    garnish

1. To toast almonds, preheat oven to 325°F. Place almonds in a single layer on baking sheet. Bake 8 to 10 minutes until golden, shaking pan or stirring occasionally to ensure even toasting. Let stand at room temperature until cool. (Almonds will darken and become crisper as they cool.)

2. Increase oven temperature to 450°F. Combine cheese, artichokes, olives, ⅔ cup picante sauce, almonds and cilantro in large bowl; mix well.

3. Brush one side of 4 tortillas with butter; place, buttered side down, on baking sheet.

4. Place 1 cup cheese mixture on top of each tortilla on baking sheet; spread to within ¾ inch of edge. Top each with 1 of the remaining tortillas, pressing firmly.

5. Brush tops of filled tortillas with butter.

6. Bake 10 minutes or until tops are lightly browned. Remove from oven. Let stand at room temperature to cool 3 to 5 minutes. Cut each quesadilla into 8 wedges.

7. Serve with additional picante sauce. Garnish, if desired.

Makes 32 appetizers

Southwestern Chilies Rellenos

4 cans (4 ounces each) whole green chilies, well drained
2 tablespoons olive oil
½ teaspoon white pepper
½ teaspoon salt
½ teaspoon ground red pepper
¼ teaspoon ground cloves
1½ cups (6 ounces) shredded Wisconsin Cheddar cheese
1½ cups (6 ounces) shredded Wisconsin Monterey Jack cheese
1 package (16 ounces) egg roll wrappers
1 egg yolk
1 teaspoon water
Vegetable oil

1. To seed chilies, cut each chili in half lengthwise using scissors or knife. Carefully scrape out and discard seeds. Rinse chilies well; drain. Pat dry with paper towels. (Wear rubber gloves when handling chilies to prevent irritation to your hands.)

2. Combine olive oil, white pepper, salt, ground red pepper and cloves in small bowl. Add chilies; toss to coat. Let stand at room temperature 1 hour. Combine Cheddar cheese and Monterey Jack cheese in another small bowl.

3. For each chili relleno, place 1 chili half in center of 1 egg roll wrapper; top with ¼ cup cheese mixture. Beat egg yolk and water in small cup; brush edges of egg roll wrapper with egg mixture.

4. Fold two opposite edges over filling, overlapping edges; press together, working out any air bubbles. Press ends together. Fold ends under and pinch to seal. Repeat with remaining chilies, egg roll wrappers and cheese mixture.

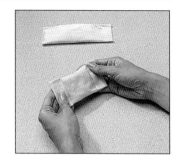

5. Heat ½ inch vegetable oil in large, heavy saucepan over medium-high heat until oil reaches 375°F; adjust heat to maintain temperature. Fry chilies rellenos, a few at a time, in hot oil 2 to 3 minutes until golden brown, turning once. Remove with slotted spoon; drain on paper towels.

Makes 6 servings

Cheesy Sun Crisps

**2 cups (8 ounces)
shredded Cheddar
cheese
½ cup grated Parmesan
cheese
½ cup sunflower oil
margarine, softened
3 tablespoons water
1 cup all-purpose flour
¼ teaspoon salt (optional)
1 cup uncooked quick-
cooking oats
⅔ cup roasted salted
sunflower kernels**

1. Beat Cheddar cheese, Parmesan cheese, margarine and water in large bowl with an electric mixer at medium speed until well blended. Add flour and salt; mix well.

2. Stir in oats and sunflower kernels; mix until well combined.

3. Shape dough into 12-inch-long roll; wrap securely in plastic wrap.

4. Refrigerate at least 4 hours. (Dough may be stored up to 1 week in refrigerator.)

5. Preheat oven to 400°F. Lightly grease cookie sheets. Cut roll into ⅛- to ¼-inch slices; flatten each slice slightly.

6. Place on prepared cookie sheets. Bake 8 to 10 minutes until edges are light golden brown. Remove immediately to wire racks. Let stand at room temperature until cool.

Makes 4 to 5 dozen crackers

Harvest-Time Popcorn

2 tablespoons vegetable oil
1 cup popcorn kernels
2 cans (1¾ ounces each) shoestring potatoes (3 cups)
1 cup salted mixed nuts or peanuts
¼ cup margarine, melted
1 teaspoon dill weed
1 teaspoon Worcestershire sauce
½ teaspoon lemon-pepper seasoning
¼ teaspoon garlic powder
¼ teaspoon onion salt

1. Heat oil in 4-quart saucepan over high heat until hot. Add popcorn kernels. Cover pan; shake continuously over heat until popping stops. Popcorn should measure 2 quarts. Do not add butter or salt.

2. Preheat oven to 325°F. Combine popcorn, shoestring potatoes and nuts in large roasting pan. Set aside.

3. Combine margarine, dill, Worcestershire sauce, lemon-pepper seasoning, garlic powder and onion salt in small bowl.

4. Pour evenly over popcorn mixture, stirring until evenly coated.

5. Bake 8 to 10 minutes, stirring once. Let stand at room temperature until cool. Store in airtight containers.

Makes 2½ quarts

Clams Casino

2 dozen medium
   cherrystone clams
8 slices bacon
1 medium onion, chopped
   (page 10)
1 green bell pepper,
   chopped
1 red bell pepper,
   chopped
1 cup butter or margarine,
   softened
¼ cup lemon juice
⅛ teaspoon ground red
   pepper
¼ cup Italian-style bread
   crumbs

1. Discard any clams that remain open when tapped with fingers. To clean clams, scrub with stiff brush under cold running water. Soak clams in a mixture of ⅓ cup salt to 1 gallon of water for 20 minutes. Drain water; repeat two times.

2. Place clams on tray and refrigerate 1 hour to help clams relax. To shuck clams, take pointed clam knife in one hand and thick towel or glove in the other. With towel, grip shell in palm of hand. Keeping clam level with knife, insert tip of knife between shell next to hinge; twist to pry shell until you hear a snap. (Use knife as leverage; do not force.)

3. Twist to open shell, keeping clam level at all times to save juice. Cut the muscle from shell and set aside top shell. Tip shell over strainer in bowl to catch clams; set aside bottom shell. Strain clam juice from bowl through triple thickness of dampened cheesecloth; reserve 3 tablespoons juice.

4. Chop clams into ¼×¼-inch pieces; set aside.

5. Using scissors, cut through several slices of bacon at once, cutting into ½×½-inch pieces.

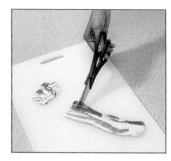

6. Cook and stir bacon in large skillet over medium-high heat until crisp. Remove with slotted spoon; drain on paper towels. Set bacon aside.

continued on page 56

Clams Casino, continued

7. Preheat oven to 350°F. Discard all but 1 tablespoon bacon drippings from skillet. Cook and stir onion and bell peppers in same skillet over medium-high heat until onion is tender but not brown. Let stand at room temperature to cool slightly.

8. Combine butter and lemon juice in small bowl; mix well. Add bacon, onion mixture and ground red pepper.

9. In another small bowl, combine clams, reserved clam juice and bread crumbs.

10. Place clam shells on baking sheets. Fill clam shells half full with clam mixture and top with 1 tablespoon butter mixture.*

11. Bake 20 minutes or until lightly browned. Garnish as desired.

Makes about 16 servings

*Clams may be frozen at this point. When ready to serve, place frozen clams on baking sheet; bake in a preheated 350°F oven for 20 to 25 minutes.

Sesame-Sour Cream Meatballs

1 medium onion
¼ cup sesame seeds,
divided
1 slice fresh bread
1½ pounds ground beef
¼ cup milk
1 egg
½ teaspoon salt
⅛ teaspoon black pepper
⅛ teaspoon ground ginger
4 tablespoons vegetable
oil, divided
4 tablespoons butter or
margarine, divided
1 cup beef broth, divided
Sesame-Sour Cream
Sauce (page 58)
Fresh Italian parsley
sprigs for garnish

1. To chop onion in food processor, peel and quarter onion; place in bowl. Pulse 4 to 7 times until onion is finely chopped. Scrape bowl once during chopping. Chop enough onion to measure ⅔ cup. Drain onions, if needed. Set aside. (See page 10 for chopping technique with knife.)

2. To toast sesame seeds, spread seeds in large, dry skillet. Shake skillet over medium-low heat until seeds begin to pop and turn golden, about 3 minutes. Set aside 2 tablespoons toasted sesame seeds for Sesame-Sour Cream Sauce.

3. Cut bread slice into quarters. Process bread quarters in food processor or blender until fine crumbs form. Crumbs should measure ½ cup.

4. Combine ground beef, onion, bread crumbs, milk, egg, salt, pepper and ginger in large bowl.

5. Place meat mixture on cutting board; pat evenly into 8×6-inch rectangle. With sharp knife, cut meat into 48 (1-inch) squares; shape each square into 1-inch meatball.

continued on page 58

*Sesame-Sour Cream
Meatballs, continued*

6. Heat 2 tablespoons oil and 2 tablespoons butter in large skillet over medium heat. Cook half the meatballs until brown on all sides, 8 to 9 minutes. Add ½ cup broth. Bring to a boil over medium-high heat. Reduce heat to low. Simmer, covered, 5 to 10 minutes. Set cooked meatballs aside. Repeat with remaining meatballs, using remaining 2 tablespoons oil, 2 tablespoons butter and ½ cup broth.

7. Meanwhile, prepare Sesame-Sour Cream Sauce. Place hot meatballs in serving bowl; top with sauce. Sprinkle with remaining 2 tablespoons toasted sesame seeds. Garnish, if desired.

Makes 4 dozen meatballs

Sesame-Sour Cream Sauce

**2 tablespoons butter or margarine
2 tablespoons all-purpose flour
½ teaspoon ground ginger
¼ teaspoon salt
½ cup beef broth
1 tablespoon soy sauce
2 tablespoons toasted sesame seeds
¾ cup sour cream**

1. Melt butter in small saucepan over low heat. Blend in flour, ginger and salt. Cook and stir until bubbly, about 1 minute. Add beef broth. Cook until thickened, stirring constantly, for an additional minute. Add soy sauce and sesame seeds.

2. Remove from heat; pour into small bowl. Add sour cream, stirring until smooth.

Makes 1½ cups

Sweet Hot Chicken Wings

1 small piece fresh ginger
1 orange
3 pounds chicken wings
¾ cup salsa
⅔ cup honey
⅓ cup soy sauce
¼ cup Dijon-style mustard
2 tablespoons vegetable oil
Additional picante sauce
Fresh Italian parsley sprigs for garnish

1. To grate fresh ginger, remove tough outer skin with sharp knife or vegetable peeler. Grate ginger using a ginger grater or the finest side of a box-shaped grater. Grate enough ginger to measure 2 tablespoons. Set aside.

2. To grate orange peel, rinse orange under running water. Grate orange peel using the finest side of a box-shaped grater, being careful to remove only the outermost layer of skin and not any of the bitter, white pith. Grate enough peel to measure ½ teaspoon. Set aside.

3. Cut off and discard wing tips from chicken. Cut each wing in half at joint.

4. Place chicken wings in 13×9-inch baking dish. Combine ¾ cup salsa, honey, soy sauce, mustard, oil, ginger and orange peel in small bowl; mix well. Pour over chicken wings.

5. Marinate, covered, in refrigerator at least 6 hours or overnight.

6. Preheat oven to 400°F. Drain marinade; reserve. Place chicken wings in single layer on foil-lined, 15×10-inch jelly-roll pan. Pour reserved marinade evenly over chicken wings. Bake 40 to 45 minutes until brown. Serve warm with additional picante sauce. Garnish, if desired.

Makes about 34 appetizers

INDEX